# SPIRITED POEMS FOR SPIRITED PEOPLE

## Betsy Brown Bass

Printed in the USA

10 9 8 7 6 5 4 3 2 1

ISBN: 978-1-955346-16-0

Cover & Layout Design: Heather Dakota
Cover Artwork by Betsy Brown Bass


Learn more at www.betsybass.com

*To all the Seekers among us*

# Spirited Poems for Spirited People

*Betsy Brown Bass*

# TABLE OF CONTENTS

# INTRODUCTION

Have you ever wanted something for a long time but didn't know how to get it or make it happen? For quite some time, I told myself I wanted to connect to the Divine, the more spiritual side of myself, but it felt elusive. I read a lot of spiritual books, studied with different teachers, attended workshops, and took online courses. In October of 2020, I joined with people from around the world in Sonia Choquette's course *Your Glorious Life*. What I love about Sonia is her authenticity and vulnerability coupled with wisdom and professionalism, so I signed up for small group mentoring as a next step.

Our first assignment was to learn something new during the week, with the goal to get in touch with our *beginner's mind* without having to be perfect. That evening, I decided to learn belly dancing, since I love other forms of dance and thought it would be fun. When I went to bed that night, I awoke and heard "you won't be doing belly dancing, you're writing poetry." It was a strange thought, but I didn't pay much attention to it and immediately fell back into a deep sleep.

About ten minutes later, the title of a poem dropped into my head, and I scrambled for a pen and something to write on. Near my tower of books on the bedside table, I kept a journal. I grabbed the journal, selected the back pages, and wrote down exactly what I heard. The poem flowed rapidly, but I kept pace. Somehow, I regulated the flow so that I didn't miss a word.

That was on January 22, 2021 at 11:55 PM and six minutes later at 12:01 AM, my poetry journey was launched. Unbeknownst to me, the back three pages of the journal already had something written on them. Fortunately, I had angled the journal slightly, so reading my poem *Meditation* was like reading crosshatch writing. Every morning, I deciphered what I had written and typed the poems from the night before. I did not want to fall behind or become overwhelmed. The poems kept flowing. I received one poem the first night, two poems for two nights. Sometimes I would receive three, four, or even five poems in one night. In all, I received 102 poems in thirty-four days.

I was overjoyed and also a bit confused by what was happening. I did not ask to write poetry, yet, I was receiving an abundance of wisdom in poetry form. The journey was certainly a wild ride. I never remembered what I wrote, and seldom recalled the titles or how many poems I wrote.

Since my husband, Mark, is a light sleeper, I tried to be as still as possible so I would not disturb him during the downloads.

Apparently I had been getting ready to be awakened numerous times during the night, but I didn't know it. For about a month before the poetry came, I woke up four to five times a night and noticed patterns of numbers on the digital clock. Numbers such as 1:23 AM, 3:33 AM, 4:32 AM or interesting combinations of numbers caught my eye. I wondered why I awoke but would go right back to sleep, not understanding or trying to figure it out either. As a pregnant woman doesn't sleep well toward the end of her pregnancy, which prepares her to wake up more easily with a newborn, I was being prepared to *birth* my poetry. When I received poems four or five times a night, I awoke, wrote the poem, and went back to sleep.

If you could have seen me writing in the middle of the night, you would have laughed because I was quite a sight. I laid on my left side with my left arm extended above me cradling my head. I kept my left eye closed hoping to remain in a liminal place between sleep and wakefulness. I scribbled the lines as fast as I received them. I learned to keep a stash of pens on the bedside table because more than once, I could tell I was merely scratching the words onto the page. I could not trust myself to recreate what I was getting if my pen ran out of ink. Not knowing why, I wrote the date and time I started and stopped writing the poem, which was fascinating to me. Sometimes I wrote for nine minutes and sometimes I wrote for twenty-nine minutes. Sometimes I fell right back to sleep for ten or fifteen minutes, and I awoke again to write more.

At first, I wrote completely in the dark and got ink on my pillowcase because I couldn't tell where the paper stopped. Ultimately, I used a small book light. Not wanting to fully awaken, I turned the light away from the paper. Having enough light to keep the pen on the paper and off my pillowcase worked perfectly.

During this entire time, I realized that the downloaded poetry was a true gift, and I couldn't control it. I relaxed and trusted the process. One day, I panicked with the thought "what if it stops?" I know that was my ego getting involved. When I thought about it, I realized if I received one poem or one hundred poems, it was all perfect. When the gift was ready to stop, it would stop, and I would say *thank you* and be grateful.

Part of receiving this gift was my readiness to be a willing vessel. When I was 24 years old, I learned Transcendental Meditation. I have meditated periodically throughout my life. In October of 2020, I became devoted to the practice, and it has become a non-negotiable. I faithfully meditate at least once and sometimes twice a day, even if only for fifteen or twenty minutes at a time. Being in a quiet, centered place on a consistent basis gave me access to my Higher Self and God. Receiving poetry as a gateway to a spiritual connection thrilled me.

The number of poems I received surprised even me. I noticed that some nights all poem titles started with the same letter. The process of writing poems never changed, and the messages were positive and uplifting ideas about love, courage, change, connection with God, oneness, nature, beauty, imagination, intuition, play, and rest.

You will notice that I use both He and She to refer to God. I ask that you substitute whatever pronouns work best for you. This is my expression of the fullness of God, which includes both the divine masculine and divine feminine. This is also how I received the poems.

I hope you are inspired by this poetry as much as I feel lucky to be the recipient of them. These poems were truly an unexpected, beautiful gift from Above. I guess I got my wish to be more connected to the Divine after all, but my connection came in an unexpected package. What are you longing for in your life? Flip through the pages of these poems, and find the answers you seek.

# INSPIRATION

# EAGLE VISION

*Started at 12:59 AM and finished at 1:17 AM*

What if our sleep is disturbed,
and we're given a new way to see,
like an eagle who soars high above
the lakes, mountains, rivers, and valleys?
He looks at the entire vista, takes in details
as small as a helpless creature below him
or as magnificent as a tall fir tree.
He flies over the grandeur of the earth,
snow-capped mountains, and clear, blue lake below.

Is he worried about what he will do,
or where he will go?
No, he is immersed in the present.
This moment is critical as he
drops to pluck a fish
from the pristine waters below.
Does he plan his day or
worry about the future?
Is he concerned about
the passage of time,
or is he focused on the now?

All he knows is the sacred essence
and fullness of this one
precious, amazing moment.
His strong wings carry him
aloft on the thermals.

He responds by instinct,
trusting what he knows.

He focuses his laser-like attention
on the present moment.
What else matters?
If he loses focus, he could
miss his next meal.
Stay the course, keep his eyes
on what he needs to see.
Does he worry about tomorrow?

He knows that life is a gift.
He is one amazing creature
fulfilling his destiny, soaring,
gliding, surveying, swooping,
and scanning high above
the clouds and raindrops.

He feels freedom, joy, and
strength course through his body
and answers the call to be himself—
the eagle who does not compare
himself to other creatures.

He is content to embrace his magnificence.
As he hearkens to a new day,
he feels the colors of dawn
burst around him.
The new day promises
challenges, hopes, adventures,
and the unknown.
Being fully his eagle self,
he trusts that he is enough.
Do we?

# WAKE UP

*Started at 5:03 AM and finished at 5:27 AM*

Will you wake up and
listen to the message,
or do you keep getting
pulled back to sleep?
How important is it to hear
what you're supposed to receive?

Perhaps you're unavailable
during the day, scurrying
from here to there.
Maybe you're totally unconscious
and prefer to fill your head with
idle gossip, reality shows, and movies.

Remember that what you
focus on will grow bigger,
so be careful to avoid fear.

Concentrate on what
you want to manifest.

If you are lost in anxiety
and self-deprecation,
then you create your
own human drama.
You contribute to your suffering
when you think that
God blames you as

a miserable sinner,
and you worry that everything
you do will be judged.

If you only knew how
gloriously, vibrantly, and fully
God loves you,
you would literally
burst with joy.

It is our human ego that
judges others and ourselves
so harshly.
God is not sitting around
keeping track of
all your transgressions.
Wake up and realize that
it is your preconceived notion
that you are not enough.

Those thoughts keep you from
a loving, nurturing conversation
with your Holy Mother and Father.
It is your birthright to
connect with your Creator.
You were divinely created
with that urge in your DNA
to bridge the gap one-on-one
to the Divinity within.

You get close sometimes,
but life is so full of distractions.
You may miss the vibration
unless you get quiet and
take time to be still.

In the nothingness or
out in the natural world,
you will be receptive.
Wake up and seek connection
through meditation, prayer, or
time outside in nature.
Wake up so you can fall deeply
into rest and peace.

# RAINBOWS

*Started at 11:57 PM and finished at 12:23 AM*

Rainbows are an alchemy of luscious
lollipop flavors: strawberry and lime,
lemon and blueberry, outlandish orange,
and a small slice of indigo.
Magnificent rainbows soften and
inspire us, and raise our hopes.

They help us realize that after
weathering something challenging,
we might receive a gift from God.
Despite the darkness of the situation,
things could possibly turn out
better than we thought.

Rainbows bring glowing
crescents of color and magic.
Sprinkle in a little fairy dust
and behold a bright, beautiful,
billowing, brilliant burst of
ridiculous color that stretches
across the sky in a hopeful arc,
leading us away from our problems,
clear to the other side with a solution.
No one can believe how
mystical rainbows can be.

They feel like misty bands of light
stretching from the clouds in

a hopeful statement that
beauty still exists,
God is home,
and we are His.
How can anything
that gorgeous even exist?
Who but God could have ever created
something so breathtaking?

Do you need a rainbow
in your life today?
Or perhaps you are a rainbow
for someone else.

Many people feel
down and discouraged,
and only notice the dark clouds
and brewing storm.
Their lives seem to be
characterized by tragedy and defeat,
and they forget that
everything is temporary.

Even if a rainbow bursts
out in front of them,
they might miss it because
their focus is filtering out
anything that could be good.

How can we be so myopic
and miss the most obvious?
If we see only with our earthly eyes,
we may miss the truth,
which is why we must learn
to expect good and know

that we will perceive and receive
the optimum when we ready ourselves,
trusting that the universe
will meet our every need.

If we can thrill in the absolute glory
and delight of a rainbow,
if we can gasp at Mother Nature's
phenomenal display of unabashed glory,
if we can expect the miraculous
and get out of our own way
enough to see it,
then we can experience
more rainbows every day.

Once we are no longer
wowed by rainbows,
we will be less likely
to see the other gifts
surrounding us all the time:
the sparkling stars in the blackest sky
and the twinkling spattering of
lights across The Milky Way.
When the first hint of dawn changes
the sky from black to dark blue
to soft pink hues, and finally
to a kaleidoscope of colors,
we could be so preoccupied,
that we don't even witness that miracle.
Without awareness, we wouldn't appreciate
the mountains deep with
purple-streaked shadows,
the misty green sea foam
splattered on the shoreline,
the bright desert flowers

blooming in unlikely spaces,
and the majestic trees as they extend
their branches toward the sky.

All of God's natural world
is a gift to inspire us,
lift our spirits, and remind us that,
like rainbows, we too are
a magnificent mix
of all the magic,
and sometimes we're
even a surprise to ourselves.

# ROADBLOCKS

*Started at 12:53 AM and finished at 1:04 AM*

What are the roadblocks
trying to tell you?
Are they a mere inconvenience and
annoyance on your way to the top?
Are they a distraction purposely
placed there to help you
pause, breathe, get centered,
and consider the next move
instead of stumbling blindly,
haphazardly down the trail?

Is the roadblock genuinely
a gift, a time out, a break
to give you a chance
to feel with your heart
and decide if you still want
to pursue that goal?
The roadblock may be a
blessing in disguise,
a way to meet
a new, precious friend,
or companion for life.

Though you may be
unsettled by the roadblock,
it may yield your greatest treasure
or the surprise of an exciting adventure.

Is the roadblock a warning,
a message to stop, simply breathe,
and determine if this
still makes your heart sing?
Is the roadblock an invitation to rest,
wait, or gather new strength
for the journey ahead?

Perhaps you created the roadblock,
but didn't know it.
You wanted to step out, step back,
create a diversion, or stop,
but you didn't know how.
The universe heard you and
delivered what you wanted.

Maybe the roadblock is a warning
from your Higher Self
that the timing is off,
the person is not right,
or the stars are not aligned.
Roadblocks teach us many things
if we wake up enough
to decipher them.

What's the roadblock in your life
communicating to you today?
Remember you've got options,
and you get to choose your actions.
If the road is blocked,
you can always strike out
in a new direction
or just stay home.

# VESSEL

*Started at 2:25 AM and finished at 2:54 AM*

What kind of vessel are you?
Are you clear and clean, ready
to hold something precious?
Are you cloudy and stained
with old liquid that never
got completely used?
Are you neglected and cracked,
chipped at the top?
Sometimes they say
the cracks allow light in.

You can be a sparkly, clean vessel,
but perhaps you would taste
too much of newness or perfection.
You would lack a certain seasoning,
not a spicy kind of seasoning,
but the feel of being seasoned
like a familiar, favorite cooking pot.

Perhaps your vessel is scratched
and worn, knocked around a bit
by life's difficulties and challenges.
Maybe your vessel is colorful and shiny,
or sturdy and steady.

Maybe your container was picked up
at a thrift store after being discarded
by previous owners as undesirable.

Maybe your vessel is part of a set,
and you function better in a group.
The actual vessel and its appearance
is less important than
the function and intention.
What is the purpose of the vessel,
and how will it be used?

First of all, we must prepare
the vessel lovingly and examine it
to see if it is suitable.
God wants us to be his vessels, so
He can fill us with the sparkling,
life-sustaining elixir of His love,
so we can pour it out on others.

He is not looking for a perfect vessel
but for an empty, available one.
If your vessel is filled with rancor,
rage, or too much religion,
there won't be enough space
for God's goodness and love,
for the sweet-flowing nectar
of His peace and the warm,
liquidy sweetness of His truth.

Do you want to be able to
join with others as they
pour out their liquid love,
goodness, and peace on a
hurting world and aching planet?
Offer yourself up as a ready vessel,
a holder of God's love.

He is not judgmental or critical,
holding you as imperfect.
Your own guilt and
lack of worthiness
cover your vessel in darkness.
God wants you now
as his vessel.
Your intention and
surrender are enough.

Empty yourself of any
doubt or fear.
Those are merely illusions.
We are the blessed and
well-loved children of God,
and He already delights in us.
We need only empty ourselves
of our ego-driven desires,
negative, self-critical ways,
and the idea that we
are separate from or
superior to our neighbors.

Will your vessel be available
as He pours out all that love
and light and goodness?

# SKELETON KEY

*Started at 4:26 AM and finished 4:41AM*

Where is the skeleton key to your life?
What happened to it?
Did you lose it along the way?
Did it fall through the
hole in your pocket
that you never fixed?
In your carelessness,
did you misplace it?
Did you give it to someone else
and forget to get it back?
Maybe you left it in the dresser drawer
and forgot you even had it.

Keys open things, and skeleton keys
purportedly open everything.
Where is the skeleton key to your life?
Did you lose it at the park, or
leave it at your friend's house?
Did you carelessly toss it in with other keys,
and now, you can't tell which one it is?

The skeleton key is magic and
holds the secret to your happiness.
It is the combination to your heart,
your motivation, the message
you want to share with the world.
Your skeleton key is not lost or
rusty, forgotten or unfound.

The skeleton key to your life is you—
you in all your glory,
you with all your warts,
you in your blazing brilliance,
you in your moments of grief,
you in your falling down and
in your rising up,
you in your loneliness and your fear,
in your boldness and in your beauty.
You are your own skeleton key.

But what is the door?
The door for the skeleton key is
the love in your heart.
You have no light without your shiny,
shimmery, bursting-with-perfection heart.
The skeleton key to your life
opens nothing unless it opens
the portal of your heart,
your greatest offering to
our world and to yourself,
your big, pure, unadulterated,
amazing, perfect heart.

You came into the world
with your nous, which means
the "eyes of the heart."
When you see with
the "eyes of your heart,"
you don't need your
skeleton key anymore.
You have everything.

# FOOTSTEPS

*Started at 12:15 AM and finished at 12:31AM*

Where were the footsteps leading?
Did they follow some well-worn path
or veer off in a new direction?
What if we followed in the footsteps?

Would we get disoriented in the snow,
losing our way in the storm?
What did the footsteps tell us?
Were the steps heavy and determined
or a light mark on the path
from one who is timid?

What if the footsteps led nowhere,
distracting us from what we need
to know, and do, and study?
Were the footsteps a temptation to
follow someone else because her words
were convincing and her attitude pure?

Did the footsteps start strong and then stop,
while the maker wandered, lost and confused?
Are the footsteps an invitation to a higher,
better place, and a purer, kinder way?
Are the footsteps made by a true leader,
a healer, a teacher who cares and wants
to share her story with others,
to help them shine their brightest lights?

Be careful whose footsteps you follow.
There are so many out there,
and they all lead different places.
Sometimes we don't really know
whose footsteps we want to follow,
but we blindly stumble down the trail.
There we are, following footsteps,
which don't ring true for us.
Don't be afraid to veer from the trail,
hop off the path, abruptly change gears.
Make sure you keep your eyes wide open.
Stay in the present moment, look around you.

What do you see?
Get centered, be in the moment,
choose to stay grounded in your body.
Now, look at those footsteps again,
and look at the maker of those footsteps.

Choose carefully and wisely.
Listen for a nudge.
Wait for the feeling of approval.
Did you get the green light?
Run, skip, jump down that path
following those footsteps.
Then, you can become the
footstep maker for someone else.

# EXPLORATION

# STARTING OVER

*Started at 2:47 AM and finished at 2:58 AM*

You won't know what to do,
and you absolutely can't rush it
because the pieces are
being laid out before you
with great care and devotion.
You must wait.

No one promised it would be easy.
You must rest, review, reflect,
and renew your visions,
quests, hopes, and big dreams.

Some people prefer to stay where
they are—wretched, rotten, and
rotting away—rather than taking a
stand for their happiness.

It does not have to be
elusive and hidden from sight,
but you may not be ready to start over.

It takes a willingness to
let go and not know.
It takes courage and conviction,
strength and innocence
to give up the familiar
and start over.

Don't be afraid.
Don't be dismayed.
Don't be discouraged.

You'll get to the starting line
at the right time.
They'll call your name, and
your backpack will be ready.

You'll tentatively take
your first step to start over,
and you won't even look back.

You won't care about the past
because you have embarked
on starting over,
and it feels really good.

# THE PORCH

*Started at 4:35 AM and finished at 4:47 AM*

When did you last enjoy
the pleasure of a porch?
Were you with your family
sharing a late-night chat?
Were you swinging on an
old-fashioned swing
that glides back and forth as
you're lulled into a slower rhythm?

Were you on a porch hoping for
your first goodnight kiss or
lingering over a long one
with your lover?

Were you visiting
with new neighbors
or sitting out there by yourself
with a hot cup of coffee
or freshly brewed tea,
staring at the wispy patterns of steam
as they formed images
in the cool morning air?

Did you come sit on the porch
seeking solace, sad from heartbreak,
or worried about
disappointing someone else?
Were you out there

sketching a landscape,
typing a novel, penning a poem,
or composing a love letter?

Were you sitting, relaxing,
allowing the porch
to transport you somewhere like
the mountains of Switzerland,
the valleys of France,
the jungles of Africa,
the deserts of the Middle East,
or the cerulean waters of Australia?

Was the porch your
passport to mind travel,
gaining access to a magical place
where all is possible and
only you hold yourself back?

If you haven't sat on a porch lately,
I hope you get to be on one soon.
It has endless possibilities for all of us.

# SECOND CHANCE

*Started at 2:03 AM and finished at 2:28 AM*

Do you wait for your life
to kick start again?
What excuse stops you from
racing off in a new trajectory,
lack of imagination and motivation,
or boredom and laziness?

Don't think you can hide now.
Today is your day.
Now is your hour.
Don't waste a precious second.
You don't know how
much time you'll have.

Each moment is a gift,
a little miracle of its own.
What will you do with
the gift of your life?

Has fear got you stuck in your tracks,
unable to move forward?
Did the inertia of the last months
keep you from evolving?

This is your chance now.
You've had a break.
The big pause button made you realize
you were spinning your wheels or

spending your precious life on minutiae.
How much has fallen away for you?
Do you really miss it,
or were you living life on
autopilot and cruise control?

Were you complacent, distracted, or
too preoccupied to notice you
were careening down a road
without a real endpoint in mind?

The chaff has been cut away.
Much of the hustling and bustling
gave way to a gentler rhythm,
a softer step, or no step at all.

Did you know how to rest
or relax before?
Did you speak to your neighbor
or have time for your friend?
Did you ever get bored enough
to imagine something unusual,
a different life, a new dream?

I hope the weariness
of your old ways
helps you break out in song
or go in unfamiliar directions.
I hope you question
all you hold dear, and
I hope your dear ones
feel your love.

Take time for yourself
because no one
will give it to you.
Guard your existence
as your biggest treasure.

Now is your chance
to explore and become
the star of your life.
Like the young child who
can be anything,
you must dust off
those childhood memories,
and reconnect to the joy
you knew back then.

What did the little kid in you
want more than anything?
Nothing stopped you from
climbing the tallest mountain
or flying a spaceship.
Nothing kept you from
being the best doctor,
saving your patients' lives.
You sailed the seas,
braved the tempests,
and starred on the stage.

You can do that again now.
The weeds along
the path of your life
have been chopped down
and cut away.
The essential roadway remains,
yet you still have to

take the first step.
What do you want to be,
and how do you
want to create the
precious pearl of your life?

# ROAD BACK HOME

*Started at 1:34 AM and finished at 1:56 AM*

When did you leave home, and why?
Was it a fight with your mother,
disagreement with your dad,
or was it time to go?

Did you leave in a huff and
slam the door on your way out?
Did you make a scene and
posture, pose, or preen?

We embarrass ourselves
with our foolishness,
foaming, fuming, and forgetfulness.
We lose touch with our roots
and toss about like dry leaves,
scrambling around the vacant lot.

We wouldn't even recognize ourselves
because we've changed so much, or
we're ashamed because
we haven't changed at all.

We never grew up and left
responsibility to someone else.
We're not proud about how we
foundered, failed, and flew away.

Sometimes we're embarrassed
about our home.
We don't like who we are
or who they were.
But it was home,
and since it was part of us,
we have to make peace with it.

We can never really leave home
because it's always part of
the fabric of our lives.
What parts do you want to keep, and
what parts are better left behind?

Save the good memories, happy times,
triumphs, and laughs.
Forgive the mistakes,
the ones you made,
and the ones they did, too.

You probably have to
leave home to understand
and appreciate it anyway.
Even if you never go anywhere physically,
you have to forge your own meaning,
make your own magic,
climb your own mountains,
and create your own dreams,
but you're never doing it alone.

Helpers, guides, and angels surround you,
watch over you, and whisper clues
about the way to go,
what you might do,
and where you can turn.

They're waiting, watching, and
will only help when you ask.

Any kind of help is available,
even if you want to go back home.
If you can't find the way,
they can guide, direct,
suggest, and soothe.

You may not know
the road back home,
but they do, and
with their assistance,
it may be time to return.

# COSTUME

What costume are you wearing now
to pretend you're someone else?
Is the mask fixed on your face, or
did it change with the play and the season?

Do you wear the cover of comedy or drama?
Is it for sport, embracing your life as
you occasionally pretend to be someone else,
a temporary role on the stage of life?

Is your costume elaborate, colorful, and fun?
Are you sinister, dark, and foreboding?
Did you enjoy going through the racks
in the vault to find the perfect one
as you adorn yourself in a
costume that reflects you?

Does the costume match your
current mood, character, or role?
Do you delight in your costume,
or is it completely covering you
to disguise your true self?

Does your costume help bring out
another facet of your sparkling personality?
Does it allow you to get in touch with
a side you don't normally express?

Does your costume encourage you to be a star,
or become an outrageous character
that you might not even like?
Does the costume make you feel
exotic, fanciful, or silly?

Does it challenge you
to develop a serious role?
By donning a costume, will you
step into the shoes of another,
experience real compassion, and
know you can go beyond yourself?

When you wear a villain's costume,
can you see that all of us
have that potential, too?
With different circumstances, scenes,
lines, script, makeup, and
a change of costume,
we could become someone else, too.

Perhaps you've judged others,
or think you're better
because you assume you could
never be like they are.
Maybe all it takes
is a change of costume.

# TRAVEL

*Started at 3:19 AM and finished at 3:38 AM*

Where do you want to go now?
Do you want to strike out
on an adventure
like walking The Camino,
or hiking the majestic
Mont Blanc in France?

Do you long to visit
the Alps of Switzerland,
ski the Italian Dolomites,
play on Maui's beaches,
swim in the Caribbean's
turquoise waters,
walk the streets of Paris,
examine the treasures
of ancient Egypt,
or marvel at wondrous animals
on a photographic African safari?

Do the bright blue lakes of Banff
or wildlife in Alaska inspire you?
Do you yearn to wander in
bustling New York City,
admire the glorious cathedrals
and churches of Europe,
join the lively shoppers along
Las Ramblas in Barcelona,
experience the sheer beauty

of the Greek isles,
be amazed by penguins and
pristine animal life of the Galápagos,
study the mystery of the Mayans, or
revel in the dizzying peaks of Machu Picchu?

Do you wish to cruise the
Rhine or Elba rivers,
lose yourself in the opulence
of the Taj Mahal,
hike the craggy shores of Scotland,
or photograph the
emerald hills of Ireland?

Do you yearn to explore the
scenic wonders of Hong Kong,
relax in the rural beauty of Thailand,
experience the cultural treats of Japan,
view the exotic treasures of Russia, or
feel the welcoming warmth of Mexico?

So many lands and so many people,
languages, cultures, foods,
and national treasures.
The riches in our world are limitless.
While obstacles can abound
outside of you,
your best travel may be to
that inward landscape.

As you are able to get quiet and go within,
you will be treated to a free ticket.
You can experience deep peace,
amazing beauty, and adventure
every time you meet yourself in stillness.

Meditation is the method.
All you need is the time, the seat,
the commitment, and the breath.
It may be your easiest mode of travel.

# SETTLE DOWN

*Started at 5:32 AM and finished at 5:43 AM*


Settle down and settle in.
What are you doing anyway?
Are you avoiding your responsibilities?
Your life is your job,
your brightest, greatest creation,
the chance to make your dreams come true.
If you don't settle down and settle in,
you could miss the whole thing.

Settle down and settle in.
Take time to decide your purpose.
Why are you here now?
What are you supposed to do?
If you don't settle down,
you may lose your way and
stumble, complain, moan, judge, and
be judged, creating chaos along the way.

Take a break, take your time,
settle down and settle in, and
wonder how you can make it better.
Take your foot off the gas,
and stop racing around.
Settle down and settle in,
and select your speed.
Get off autopilot and cruise control.

Settle down and settle in,
and choose a destination.
It doesn't really matter where.
Pick a place.
It doesn't have to last forever,
but settle down and settle in,
and be part of the process of your life.
Even if you only stay at that destination
one hour, at least, you chose.

Settle down and settle in,
and choose again.
Don't be tossed around on
a sea of uncertainty,
feeling like a victim,
shipwrecked on the beach,
flung up salty and
cold on the shore.
Settle down and settle in.
Take the helm, grab the wheel,
chart your course.

It doesn't matter if you sailed
into the wrong harbor.
There are things to be learned
everywhere and every time.
Settle down and settle in,
and select again.

# IMAGINATION

# THE MAGICIAN CARD

*Started at 3:22 AM and finished at 3:39 AM*

The infinity symbol flashes across my eyelids
reminding me that all is possible.
Like the Magician card
from the ancient Tarot,
we can be our own magic-maker and creator.

The Magician holds aloft a magic wand
and intuits that he is
surrounded by all he needs—
Wands and fire to create and inspire,
Cups to navigate emotions and
connect to our feminine side,
Swords to cut through thoughts and
release what we no longer need,
Pentacles to be practical and
to make our life work.

We have all the elements.
We have beauty and imagination,
and anything is possible.
We are often surrounded by gifts,
but we miss what is available.
Our planning and preconceived notions
block the magic of the moment.

The Magician weaves spells
and conjures what he needs.
His imagination is a willing partner

in the creation.
He dreams, plays, pretends,
and spins straw into gold.

The alchemy of his imagination and
unlimited possibilities of his creativity
provide a joyful, freewheeling spirit
for making something from nothing,
an imaginative masterpiece
in the mind's eye,
a joyful focus of the heart,
a commitment to create
and let go of the results.

Join with God, the angels,
your muse, guides, and your own
divine, wild spirit inside
to unleash your own Merlin
and become the mystical magician
and masterful wizard of
the life you desire.

Move the mountains, crash the waves,
paint the sky with bold brushstrokes.
Free your inner Magician,
burst forth with joy and
unfettered enthusiasm as you
become the artist of your life,
the playwright of your script,
the dancer flying across the floor,
turning pirouettes in space.

You emblazon your life
with love, joy, and wonder
because you are a Magician.

# CINDERELLA

*Started 12:56 AM and finished 1:11 AM*

Will you allow yourself to be
like Cinderella, a poor girl who
clung to her dream despite
hardship, meanness, poverty, and pain?
She could have been bitter,
focused on the ashes.

Did she complain and succumb
to her own disappointment?
Did discouragement design
her life and actions?

No, she rose above the
illusion of her situation.
In her heart, she was a princess.
Her meager outer trappings
never stopped her heart
from wishing and her mind
from mystery and magic.

The super power of imagination
gave her wings to fly
above the situation,
not tethered to Earth by
the reality others saw.

She dared to create her own reality,
spinning a magical tale of

beauty and delight,
using the elements available
to her and asking her
Fairy Godmother for help.

Did she know how the prince
would fall in love with her?
Did she believe that mice could be
transfigured into horses
or a garden pumpkin transformed
into an elegant coach?
Did she have to understand magic words
or analyze how it transpired?

No, she clung to her vision
and accepted without a doubt
that she would get her dance
and find her prince.
Did she suffer when the
clock struck midnight,
and the magic seemed to disappear?

No, Cinderella held firm and strong
despite the problems,
even with unfair treatment
from her stepmother and stepsisters.
She worked and kept her head down,
while her heart burst with belief.

Cinderella never gave up on herself.
She never gave up on her dream,
her desire, her destiny.
Do you have it in you, Cinderella?

# WHAT IF?

*Started 1:34 AM and finished 1:55 AM*

What if I'm someone else,
a me I no longer recognize?
What if all preconceived images
must fly away like birds migrating
as they honk noisily in the sky overhead,
starting on a journey to somewhere?

What if I am led to a place
my inner spirit knows?
What if I am transported by my soul
who knows the path by heart, guided by
unseen forces deep within me that
stir, move, call, and direct me?

What if the destiny doesn't matter,
but the journey becomes an adventure?
What if I create new formations, and
I lead, or I am led by others
as we take our turn
in front and make the way
easier for others?

What if we magically know when
to move into that lead position,
and then, when we are tired,
slip back into formation,
not knowing or caring that
we were blazing the trail or

setting the course?
We were flying by moonlight
and following our hearts,
guided by forces
bigger than our own.
We were off on a new adventure
of an old kind of story,
a different chapter of ourselves
that we had yet to write.

What if the twirling colors
around us became us,
and we were formed into
magnificent creations
we did not even recognize?

What if the journey had us
tumbling, flying, and
whooshing through space,
feeling our glory as we
all became one body
of love, light, and goodness?

What if migratory patterns took us
swirling through the heavens
as we tumbled through the clouds,
and our patterns made
new lacy clouds in the sky?

What if our souls knew when to go,
and we were just along for the ride?

# ABLE

*Started at 4:50 AM and finished at 5:07 AM*

Are you able and capable of
doing what is required?
Are you steady and
ready for the pace?

Are you able to
step up to the rigors
of writing every day or
listening to the Muse
when she comes calling
at the strange dark hours
of the morning?

Will you answer the
call to creativity,
which is God's way to
free you from your captivity?
Does your soul yearn to
stretch, grow, learn,
experience, and make mistakes?

To be fulfilled, your
Spirit must listen.

Are you able to feel the
stirrings of your soul
and heed the littlest nudges
to pick up a pen,

grab that paintbrush,
mold the sculpture,
make up a tune, or
craft the words to a song
that pierces or soothes another soul?

Are you able to put aside
comfort, convenience, and busyness
to make room for the essential?
Are you able to feel more fully alive
by responding to the urges within?

When you do, your spirit will soar,
your hope will be renewed,
your body will thank you,
and you will quiver with excitement
as you reconnect body, mind, and spirit.

Are you able to proceed
without knowing the outcome
of the final product?
When you create,
you release the real magic.

Those little bubbles of joy
bounce all over the atmosphere
and free other souls to let
loose of their creativity.
Rainbow-colored, clear
reflecting spheres of joy
float up and rise elusively
until they burst.

As they travel, you can't help
but squeal with delight
as your eyes follow, and you
want to catch them in your hand.

You, now, in your creativity cloak,
are like that bubble that
we all want to follow.
Are you able to let your
soul's whispers stir you to action?

Will you allow deep yearnings
to become crazy, new,
outlandish creations?
If you're able, we'll thank you
because we want to say
we're able, too, and
like the iridescent bubbles,
we want to rise and
float away, not knowing
how high we'll go.

# WILLING

*Started at 5:50 AM and finished at 6:02 AM*

Are you willing to be fully conscious?
Will you set aside all urgings
but your own desire to create?
Will you pay attention to signs,
listen to clues, and
make room for yourself
in the busy room of your mind?

Are you willing to be a beginner?
Are you willing to fail?
Are you willing to experiment,
color outside the lines,
and carve a different pathway?

Are you willing to go alone
and not care if your friends
call you crazy?
Are you willing to take a stand
for yourself and your right to create
for joy and adventure?

You may not know how
to navigate the twists and turns.
Just like a wild ride down the rapids,
trust that you will be guided
past the big boulders and other dangers.

Are you willing to surrender and
allow your inner child
the space he needs,
the time he craves, and
also your attention,
so he feels understood and adored?

Are you willing to suspend judgment
and simply trust that it is in
making, creating, drawing, acting,
painting, cooking, singing,
and rhyme-making
that your soul can fly free again
and spin those ribbons of
joy, laughter, love, and delight
into wondrous, bold, bountiful gifts
for yourself and for the world?

Will you join in?

# IMAGERY

*Started at 7:22 AM and finished at 7:38 AM*

Do you think in full-length,
colored movies—
double and triple features?
Do the colorful photos
flash through your mind?
Can you catch them as they go by?

Do you take time to see, feel,
experience, taste, and touch them?
The more real you can make
an experience in your mind,
the easier it will be to
manifest that dream.

The more you can make it
vivid and vibrant,
spinning with color, feeling,
and excitement,
the more easily you can
call it to you.

All life is vibration,
energy, and frequency.
Our thoughts create a picture,
an image, a desire.
We dress up our thoughts
with emotion to
magnetize the desire.

In our imagination,
we touch it,
taste the sweet nectar,
and hear a mystical melody,
the song of our heart's desire.
All the imagery weaves
into a golden tapestry
of desire, magic, and mystery.

Riding creativity's wave engages us
almost as much as the dream.
Imagery is life.
The more proficient you become
at designing thoughts that tingle
with richness, fulfillment, and excitement,
the better your real life will be.

You won't be shaking up a snow globe,
looking inside at a magical scene.
You will be living in the middle of
the swirling snowflakes of whatever
scene you have birthed into being.

Imagination, creativity, and
imagery hold the key.

# MAGIC CARPET RIDE

*Started at 3:55 AM and finished at 4:04 AM*

Are you ready to travel on
a magic carpet ride?
Are you ready for a journey?
Are you free enough to hold on
and tune in to see where
a magic carpet ride will take you?

Are you a famous opera singer
hitting high notes?
Are you a rockstar playing bass
at a frenzied rock concert?

Where can a magic carpet ride take you?
Do you soar above cities, and
dip into the valley,
swirl next to a waterfall, and
plunge close to a chasm?

Are you eager for a magic carpet ride
of your mind?
Your imagination is the originator
and wizard of your ride.

When did you last let your
inner Magician be in charge?
Will a magic carpet ride
transport you heavenward
to see stunning views and

experience massive beauty?
Are you ready for a magic carpet ride?
No need to be afraid.
Hang on.
It's easier than you think.
If you're ready for the
thrills, chills, and maybe spills,
a magic carpet awaits you,
so you can be the dream weaver
and artistic designer of your life.

Are you ready for a magic carpet ride?
Get on. It's time.

# RESTORATION

# Sea Foam

*Started at 2:12 AM and finished at 2:23 AM*

What happens to particles
left in sea foam?
Are they recycled back
to the sea, or do they
spin and spit themselves
out on the shore?
What happens to lovely
pieces of seaweed
trapped in little eddies
at the ocean's edge?
So many mysteries and
so many questions.

Are we like the foamy
pieces of debris
scattered here, there,
and everywhere?
What happens to us
as we lose our focus
and can't find our way?

Did we lose sight
of our dream?
Did we veer off course
like a shipwrecked boat
that crashed on the sand bar,
sailing too close to the shallows?

What keeps us on track
or helps us sail
straight to our mark?
Why do we lose the way,
drop the compass,
or feel bereft of any help?

Sometimes we imagine
that we are abandoned,
forgotten, and forsaken.
How do we forget so easily
that we are never alone?

Love guides and nurtures us,
providing what we need, but
perhaps not what we desire.
Love, that powerful, unexplained
source of the universe
that protects, prompts,
and nudges us,
never forsakes us.

Love is our leader, our lamplight,
our way out of the lost places.
Love is the ever patient mother
and determined father,
the softness of an eyelash
and the strength of the sea.

Love restores and gives life.
Love remembers us when we
can't even remember ourselves.
Love. Light. Love.
You're not lost after all.

# A DATE WITH YOURSELF

*Started at 4:15 AM and finished at 4:33 AM*

Do you wine and dine yourself?
Do you romance yourself
and buy roses?

Do you invite yourself
into intimate conversations,
so you delight in your own company?

How do you treat yourself?

Are you constantly nagging
and criticizing everything?
Your appearance, body, clothes,
mind, actions, and reactions?

Do you treat yourself with
kindness and respect,
tenderness and love?

Do you whisper soft words
of encouragement and cheer
from the sidelines?

Do you accept and love yourself,
which encourages you
to go beyond the comfort zone?

Do you make time to unwind
and watch your favorite movie?

Do you move your body even though
you are weary from work
and stressed out from the world?

Do you sit quietly, sink into a chair,
and let the day's worries melt away
as you pray and empty your mind?

Do you feed yourself
vibrant, healthy food,
so your body can be strong,
and also allow yourself
an occasional sweet treat
and deviation from the norm?

Do you stimulate your heart and mind?

Read poetry, fascinating novels,
adventure stories, and fairy tales.
Paint, sketch, sculpt, or
play with color to feed your soul
and delight your spirit.

Sing and dance wildly to connect
to your roots and stomp
to ground yourself in your body.

Play with your pets and soak up
the sweet, pure love of animals
who ask nothing but
our willingness to connect.

Venture out into nature
to hike, climb, walk, or run,
so your body feels your heart beat,
and you know you're alive.

Remember that no one else
is going to come and rescue you.

# DIVORCE

*Started at 5:16 AM and finished at 5:33 AM*

It's not leaving a marriage and
changing a family.
In this kind of divorce, you leave
and abandon yourself.

You could be divorcing yourself for
someone else in a myriad of ways.
You might cut yourself off
and ignore your own life.
Go into your inner temple
to replenish and rebuild.

You could be divorced from yourself
because you are too obsessed
with your children and their lives.
You forget that you must
have your own life as well.

Your job might be holding your rage
or at least that is the lie
you tell yourself.
Is the money, power, pressure,
and prestige worth
losing your precious self?

What else keeps you from yourself?

Too many activities, even if
they are designed to create good?
Too many classes or online courses?
Too many meetings or phone calls?
Too many committees or volunteer hours?

Too much anything prevents you
from being with yourself in
that meditation chair or
taking a stress-reducing walk.

Focus on yourself.
Drop out of your head
and into your heart.
Claim time to feel free,
safe, grounded, and whole.

Meet yourself where
the angels hover
and gently guide you
back to your true self.

If you've been divorced
from yourself for a while,
consider coming back
to wholeness.
Perhaps you lost your way
or got caught up in labels.
Travel the path back to yourself
and leave that divorce behind.

# REST

*Started at 12:17 AM and finished at 12:31 AM*

Are you getting profound
and abiding rest,
so that your soul and
spirit are refreshed?
Do you know the deep
peace of meditation
where your body and
soul drop down within,
allowing your spirit
a much needed
time off from worry?

Does your body know
true rest, the kind that comes
after using it well—
moving, dancing, stretching,
playing, and reaching?
That feeling of muscles being taxed
and huge soul-stirring breaths
of oxygen fill your lungs
rather than the tiny sips
of air you normally take?

Does your spirit know how to rest,
to be by the waterside, and
allow the refreshing,
rhythmic movement wash away
the debris of fear and doubt?

Does your mind know how to rest,
so you don't endlessly
run it in circles,
unproductively circling the wagons
on the same problem
over and over?

When the plane of your mind
cannot land but keeps
circling the airport
unable to land because of
the foul weather that
clouds your mind and
does not allow it to rest?

Can you rest in the comfort,
conviction, and character
of who you are?
Do you rest in your authentic,
vulnerable self, the one
you are designed to know,
and the one who can rest
in who he is without
any rehearsals or practice?

Can you rest and celebrate in the
incredible gift you are to the world,
in your own God-given beauty,
and your special way of walking,
talking, and sharing your talents?

Please rest in the acceptance
and love of self.
When you learn to rest
in the gift of yourself,
you will step up and
serve yourself
to the world and to others, too.

Rest in yourself.
Rest in God's love for you.
Then, you can show others
how to rest as well.

# THE MUSIC WITHIN

*Started at 6:11 AM and finished at 6:22 AM*

Can you hear your own song,
the one that calls you home
and back to self?

The inner music has no
particular beat or melody
and no predictable chords.
Its secret messages
fuel your destiny.

Did you lose your song
through overwork and
too many activities?
Did the time fade away
because you were too busy
listening to the music of others
or the distractions of life?

Did you forget to return home
to self a few hours a week
and refresh the melody?
It's never too late.
Put down your to-do list.
Take off the headphones.
Turn off the outer music.
Hear the gentle call of the birds
and the wind murmuring in the trees

calling you home to yourself
where the music is the sweetest.

The beat you feel is truest because
you have come home to yourself
to hear the music within.

# RETREAT

*Started at 5:27 AM and finished at 5:47 AM*

Do you need to go on a retreat
where you can treat yourself well?
Take a timeout in the best way.
Are you weary from politics
and the news?
Step away from the world
to step into yourself.

What is missing in your life now?
Peace of mind, rest, and
relaxation for your body?
A tonic for your soul
where you can
journal, draw, and dream?
Your body will thank you
as you dance freely
across the meadow,
sweat on a rigorous hike,
detoxify with crystal water,
fresh juices, and light food.

Does your mind need
a cleanse, too,
washed clear by the rushing
brook of silence?
The sun of pure nothingness
can bake and bleach away
splotches and stains

of regret, loss, and anger.
Deep rivers of grief
no longer drown you,
but their soft, salty waters
cover you, and retreat from you,
taking the aching sorrow,
guilt, and regret and
leave only sparkling nuggets
of lessons learned.

Would a retreat be
what you need to get
the creative juices flowing
once more?
You don't need a fancy spa
for a retreat.
Why don't you do that
for yourself now?
Can you carve out space at home?

What do you need
for your retreat?
You need time, time to be alone,
to reflect, to listen, to nap,
to walk, dance, and sweat.
Time to pray and sing.
Time to practice yoga
and take deep breaths.
Time to be empty, so empty
that God can easily fill
your well instead of
searching for ways to get in.

On your retreat,
allow your body to heal,
give you directions,
set the course,
and chart the day.
How well have you listened?
Has your body been asking you
to move, stretch, and strengthen,
and stop stuffing and indulging?
Has your body been
stiff and unyielding
because your spirit has, too?

Your body is your messenger
and holds wisdom.
Please meet your body
on your retreat.
Let your mind come, too,
but tell it that it's not
in charge this time.
To your spirit, send the
biggest, brightest balloons
in your spirit's favorite color.
Tie on ribbons and
bring roses, too.
To sweeten the deal,
promise your spirit chocolate
as a treat.
After all, this retreat is
for all of you—
mind, body, and soul,
and your spirit
is the honored guest.

# READY

*Started at 4:35 AM and finished at 4:48 AM*

Are you ready to fly
like the wind,
careening only
into yourself?
Why would you want
to be anyone else?
Are you ready to show up
and play full out?

We need to take
our little kid selves
and thrill them.
Hold tea parties,
draw in the sand at the beach,
run with wild abandon,
play make-believe.

Live free with joy and experience
the full range of emotions.
Maybe you are weathering a storm,
and things seem chaotic
and out-of-control.
Don't be afraid to feel
those messy feelings.

You are never alone, and
even if God has not
answered your prayers

the way you expected,
He is still there for
comfort and direction.

As you delve deeper into
the gift of yourself,
ideas will pop into your head
and inspiration will come
to you in unforeseen ways.
Keep asking for what you want,
what you need, what you
wish to understand.

Keep asking for love, joy,
peace, and strength.
When you are ready,
you may find
the answers reside inside you.

# TRANSFORMATION

# MEDITATION

*Started 11:55 PM and finished at 12:01 AM*

The magic place of nothingness
is filled with relief
as I tumble into my chair.
Preparations delay me once more.
I light the candle,
burn the incense,
and clang the Tibetan bowl
to honor the day's
most important appointment,
the one thing
I claim for myself.

Meditation calls to me
from deep inside my soul,
a moment to step out of self,
an invitation to
drop deeply into self.
I fidget in my chair,
pulling the weighted blanket
up to my chin to help
ground the flighty part of me
and anchor me to sit.

Waves wash over me as
colored lights dance on my eyelids.
Indigo and bold, lemon yellow
morph into geometric images,
and my mind drifts in and out,

a thought here, and then,
Nothing.

Melting deeper and deeper into
the quiet oasis of my heart,
here I meet God, self, nothingness,
and everything.
Peace, possibility, vulnerability,
and strength.

# FALLING

*Started at 1:10 AM and finished at 1:24 AM*

Are you falling up?
Are you falling out?
Are you falling apart,
so you can finally
fall together?
Falling feels frightening,
yet it is simply
another point of view.
What if up is down
and down is up,
and they are both sideways?

What if it is all an illusion
except God's direction?
What if all of this falling
is to fall into Her or
the divine essence of ourselves?
What if we have to break apart
the old to truly come together
in the wholeness of our being?
What if we have made it all up,
and the story's not that good?

What if the cracking of
our old shell allows the glory
of our inner selves
to radiate through?

What if our inner light
could not show before
because it was covered
with layers of inauthenticity?

What if we became vulnerable,
got scrambled up, mixed around,
reshaped, and reborn?

What if our light couldn't shine
out from under the costume
of our false selves,
but we needed to break apart
so much that we almost
couldn't recognize ourselves?

Like a kaleidoscope
of rearranged shadows,
now we can emit light
where before there was only
posturing to please others.

Did we prostrate ourselves
before the false idols of
acceptance, applause, and appetite?
What if we had to fall
to be caught,
and our breaking apart
is really our coming together
in love with no limits,
just love?

# RIVER

The river flowed gently,
sweeping along debris.
The river meandered through the meadow
gracefully lapping the earth as
wildflowers danced nearby.
The river rushed, gushed,
and foamed over,
her impatience slapping the banks
as she barreled toward the sea.

The power of the river is
like our emotions,
at times gentle, or
wild, free, and bold,
crashing the shore or
beating upon the rocks,
out of control, destroying
everything in its path.
Do our emotions run us, or
do they define us?
Will we let them have
their way with us,
or shall we rein them in?

Water's force rips people
and places apart,
and our emotions
can do the same

when we lash out in fury.
Water carves a deep rut
in a hillside and
drowns everything in sight.
Untethered and unfettered,
it can rip and rake the land.
Do our emotions race away
with options and slam the
riverbanks of our lives with
fury, fomentation, and foolishness?

What can we learn from the river?
It can wash, clean, and purify.
It can cover ugliness
and leave freshness
where once barrenness
reflected emptiness.
It can be swift, powerful,
terrible, or terrifying.
It can destroy, leaving
devastation and pain, and
render some places unrecognizable.

May the emotions we feel
run through us like the river,
but not define, limit, engulf, or
destroy and leave us
like naked branches,
bare on the bank.

# LIFE,
# THE PROOFING BOWL

*Started 2:16 AM and finished 2:29 AM*

We are all a bit like
newly rising bread.
Add the flour, salt, and yeast.
Mix with water and wait.
Wait for us to rise, grow,
and become filled with little
bubbles of alchemy and change.
The mystery of the yeast
puffs out the dough,
cushioning it with air,
allowing it to rise.

As it grows, it changes.
The enchantment of bread dough,
the magic of man and woman.
What experiences push
and pull you,
causing you to change?

Will you allow the shape
of yourself to grow and stretch,
becoming soft, pliable,
elastic, smooth, and supple?
You are no longer just
your original ingredients of
flour, salt, water, and yeast.

As if by magic, you have
become a new creation.
With the proper conditions,
the yeast will proof,
and the dough will rise
like a magical mountain,
a soft, supple dome,
a mystical creation
arising out of dust and liquid.

With care and the
right conditions,
we too will rise up
like bread dough
and become edible,
useful, helpful, and pure.
From the nothingness
of ourselves,
our Spirits enter and
fill our hearts,
and we transform,
filled with life-giving breath.

We rise up from our
stagnant, ego-driven lives
to become better
examples of ourselves,
transition into alluring,
tasty versions of the mere
ingredients we were before,
become our own masterpieces,
and hopefully are consumed,
enjoyed, and shared.

# LIGHTNING

*Started at 2:39 AM and finished at 2:49 AM*

Lightning jolts us out of our rut,
catapults us out of laziness and
shocks us with its power.
Its light is a burst,
a zing of electricity,
static movement, and might.
Do we sit around
like uncaring bystanders
ignoring the majesty of it all,
missing the mystical light show
of divine intervention?

Where do you want
a lightning bolt in your life?
Do you need to be
awakened from the reverie
of your dull, boring life?
Are you stuck in quicksand
with the nothingness
of your purpose?
Day-to-day, are
you sleepwalking through life,
dragging the cement boots
of your problems with you?

Will you let go
like the lightning and
be blown by the wind,

whipped around by
the unseen forces trying to
snap you out of your inertia?

What will it take to
wake you up to your
one great, glorious life?

Do you require
a blast of lightning?
It won't be necessary if you
look for the signs,
pay attention to help
the Universe sends your way.

Do you miss the clues,
gifts, and surprises
because you're watching and
think guidance has to
come in a special way?
There's love, light, and
help everywhere.

Will you be nudged softly
from your slumber?
Will you hear the
tiny whispers and catch
the angels' floating feathers,
signs that they are
truly with you?
Or do you need that
crack of lightning?

# CROSSING

*Started at 2:17 AM and finished at 2:39 AM*

Are you ready for the crossing,
a time of transition when you
just don't know anymore?
You don't know anymore,
and you can't know any more
because your life is breaking apart,
creating a better, higher,
different way. And
everything is brand new.

Don't try to figure it out
because it won't
change a thing.
You might miss the mystery,
melancholy, magnificence,
and mind-altering changes,
which will shake you up and
break you out of your old ways.

People don't like to give up
what they get used to having,
so sometimes the change
must be rapid and
the crossing abrupt.

What will happen to you
as you face the crossing?
You might plunge ahead,

throwing yourself face first
into the ocean
of the unknown.

When you see the
vastness of the crossing,
you may stand and shiver
at the shore, dip in a toe,
and become more hesitant
all the time.

You may want a guarantee, and
until you have one in writing,
you freeze like a statue
in a child's winter game.

As you face the crossing,
you lament what you will
miss if you cross.
You worry about the outcome
and wonder how
you can turn back,
or you start the crossing
and panic because you can't
predict what lies on
the other side of the arroyo.

What's the best way
to handle the crossing?
Do so with grace, gratitude,
grit, and a grin.
You'll have more fun,
and you might as well
have a great attitude.
Who wants to cross

with a grouch, a grinch,
or a grizzly bear?

Just relax, take your time,
enjoy the view,
look out into the valley,
breathe in the pure,
fresh mountain air.
The creativity of the crossing
can be whatever you desire,
so why not create a
blockbuster ending with
smooth sailing the entire voyage,
a stellar crew, and paradise
as the perfect endpoint?

After all, the crossing
is up to you.
The Universe can help
you get there,
but nobody can
do your pushups for you.
Pick up your feet,
and put them down,
one after the other.

Unseen forces of good
will probably be holding you.
So even if you look down,
lose your balance, or
change your mind,
you will be held aloft
until you can regain
your footing and get ready
to finish the crossing.

# THE HIGHER CALLING

*Started at 1:58 AM and finished at 2:14 AM*

Will you answer the higher calling
or ignore it?
Do you hide like a turtle
in its shell to escape
from the stirring, shaking,
and breaking apart
from your reality?
Are you called to
give up bad habits?

Why do you resist change?
In the natural world,
leaves turn bright,
glorious jewel tones
and flutter from the trees.
The moon waxes and wanes,
and fills your heart
and the sky with
desires and dreams.

The temperature drops
and cold winds give way
to softer breezes and
warmer temperatures.
Birds who disappeared in winter,
return with joyous choruses
as they herald a new beginning.
Nature is your biggest teacher.

If you learn from Her,
you accept that
nothing stays the same.
Crops grow and get harvested.
Eggs hatch and new
creatures take to the skies.
They follow their instinct
to become what
they were created to be.
They have to change.

You, too, must change.
Pay attention to the
whispers on the wind.
Notice the slightest discomfort
in your old ways.
Do you need to take
some action steps,
or do you numb yourself out
with pills, food,
distraction, or drink?

Craft the greatest
version of yourself.
Listen, go within;
make space and time.
Don't expect another
expert to answer
the questions you need to ask.
No one knows more than you do.

You're not in this precious life
by yourself, even if
you feel abandoned.
You run from your calling

or raise the volume of
busyness so much that
you can't hear anything internal.

Do you drown out
your own calls,
the ones to yourself?

Put down the distractions
of your life, and
get into a rhythmic beat.
Wake with the sun,
stretch, and breathe.
Be quiet. Don't fill
every waking moment
with outside information.
That won't help you change.

Keep the appointment
with yourself to find *your*
delight, movement, and joy.
If you do, you won't
mind the change,
and you can heed
*your* higher calling.

# UNIFICATION

# COWS

*Started at 5:23 AM and finished at 5:33 AM*

I've never particularly
been a fan of cows,
probably the city girl in me,
my lack of knowing them
and seeing into their souls.
They seem loud, ponderous,
big, bulky, noisy, and
a little bit scary.

For the cow lovers among us,
I apologize now.
I have been told that
some people love cows.
They see them as sweet,
gentle, and approachable.
So why not for me?

Ignorance, lack of experience,
judging, deciding ahead of time
that I am not a lover of cows.
But, what if I could be
open, empty, receptive,
and curious?

What if I made space
to be different?

What if I dropped
everything I thought to
be true about myself and
became an empty vessel?
What if light pours into me,
sweeps through me, and
clears away all prejudices
and ideas about who I am,
what I like, and
what I will tolerate?

What if all things
become possible,
and I flat-out don't
know myself anymore?
What if, after opening,
I become the biggest
cow lover ever?

I touch soft ears, gaze
into fringe-covered eyes,
and recognize another soul.
I feel their beating hearts
and really let them in.

I see with the
eyes of my heart, and
cows are captivating.
What if I've been wrong
about cows all along and
because I am different,
so are they?

# REFLECTION

What do you reflect upon?
Does your soul yearn
to do something?
What about your
relationships, path, career?

Do you bounce out of bed
in the morning,
eager to start your day
with a song in your heart
and rhythmic dance
in your body, or do you
drag yourself day-to-day
to make ends meet?

At work, do you feel helpful,
wanted, and important?
Sometimes we have
temporary stopping off places
or jobs that serve as
stopgaps to help us get by
until we really plug into
our soul's passion.

What about the
reflection of your life?
If you look into the mirror,
do you reflect beauty,

shimmering like the sun?
Will you express gratitude, grace,
and joy to be alive?

What does your reflection
tell others about you?
You are worthy, and
others also deserve dignity,
respect, kindness, and truth.

What do you want
your reflection to be
as you gaze upon
the waters of your soul?

Do you reflect a clear,
peaceful, and vulnerable self?
If so, then you are
an authentic mirror.
As you share the reflection
of your precious spirit,
you encourage others
to do the same.

In this way, we all become
reflections of one another.

# REMEMBER

*Started at 3:05 AM and finished at 3:23 AM*

Remember that everything
you do affects others.
You are not an island
unto yourself though you
may choose to operate
as if you are the
only one around.
Every single thought, action,
inaction, and word
ricochets in the universe
like a billiard ball
loosened as it bounces
around the table.
We can't imagine how
our thoughts affect others,
but they do.

How often do you direct
unkind, unforgiving thoughts
toward your neighbor?
Do you feel wronged, ignored,
confused, or hurt by them?
Do you retaliate by creating
fantasies about how everyone
is out to get you?

You set up a force field
of negativity, and you
magnetize the environment
to return the same to you.

We are not in control
of everything, but
remember that your
intention and expectation
of a situation color
the shade of the outcome.

Remember that it is
possible to have a change
of heart and attitude.
Extend patience, kindness,
understanding, and grace
to your fellow traveler.
You can't comprehend
what obstacles have been strewn
onto their path today.

Remember that you
don't know their story.
How do they suffer?
What sadness do they carry?
What disappointment
eats away at them?

Remember that you
create your life everyday,
and you imagine stories
about others as well.
You might as well err
on the side of kindness.

Isn't this the gift we want
extended to us?
Could we offer it to others
instead of cursing them or
assuming the worst?
Remember that your wholeness
and holiness bless them.

As we spread kindness
and love,
remember that we bathe
in the same force field
of the mercy and
positivity we crave.

# RESPECT

*Started at 3:36 AM and finished at 3:51 AM*

Respect is a gift you
bestow on others
but forget to give
to yourself.
Start with yourself or
respect won't evolve.
Respect means not judging,
not knowing, and not
predicting any kind of
behavior from others.

Erect boundaries for yourself,
so others can't intrude to
stomp on your emotions like
some out-of-control elephant,
rampaging through the jungle.
We all desire respect.
We discuss it, but
do we offer it to others?

What does it feel like
to reflect respect?
It means you carry yourself
aloft, erect, proud, but
humble at the same time.
You trust yourself, and
don't lash out at others.

You wear respect as
a newly laundered shirt,
clean, fresh, but not
too stiff with starch.

Your self-respect allows you
to assume the best of
your sisters and brothers.
Respect means not
tromping on someone else,
not on their feelings, property,
ideas, or spirit.

Respect means you treat
animals with kindness and care.
When we respect everyone
and everything, we teach
others to respect us.
Then, we all feel safe to
express our unique selves.

# RECEIVE

*Started at 3:18 AM and finished at 3:45 AM*

Are you ready to receive?
Be ready for abundance.
Be ready for God's blessings
because they are gifts.

She's not up there in the sky
keeping track in a big ledger
to see if you deserve them.
Blessings are Her gift to you
because you are Hers.

She loves you and
wants you to prosper.
Be joyful, sing, and
share your blessings to
enhance the lives of others.
Are you ready for the gift,
or are you sitting around
in sackcloth and ashes,
beating yourself up for
your lack of progress
and perfection?

You are God's gift to Herself
and the world.

Don't squander yourself
and waste your precious life
in petty meanness, jealousy,
strife, or misthinking.

Thinking causes trouble
because most of the time
you're making it up and
getting it all wrong.
Your neighbor is not
always out to get you.

If we love you as you are,
then we can be accepted, too.
You don't have to wait
to receive until you think
you're good enough.

You were born perfect,
and those scratches, stains,
bumps, and scars make
you unique and able to accept
the flaws in others.
Your humanness draws
people to you
and helps heal them.
When we receive the gift
of acceptance and love
from others, we access
more love for ourselves.

The well is never dry, and
we are all in a big cycle of love.
Receiving is not that difficult,
but you may be holding back.

*Mea Culpa*, "It's my fault"
you say, and you block
the ability to receive.
When you can be open
and ready, clear with
your intention, and steadfast
in your prayers, you are
devoted enough to receive.

It's not about whether you're
worthy enough to receive,
but are you ready?
Will you have gratitude,
sweet as a luscious, full rose
bursting with perfume,
its headiness spreading
in a wide radius?

Gratitude will enable
you to receive.
Like a small child whose
hands are open for a surprise,
a gift, you too will be ready
because gratitude has primed
the pump of preparedness.

Will you receive the blessings now?
The Divine Feminine with
her fluttering robes of pink
compassion and love is ready
to cover your life with
softness, ease, carpets of
wildflowers for your Soul,
and a sweet balmy

fragrance of jasmine, citrus,
or pine for your Spirit.

The Divine Feminine will
help you receive.
The time to receive is now.
Your precious life matters,
and we need your power,
production, and passion.
It all works together to make us one.

When you make yourself
ready to receive, then
the love keeps spilling over
like an overflowing fountain.
Receive now, so
God can give you even
more of Herself because
when you have that,
you have it all,
the divinity of
your true self.

# ON THE STAGE

*Started at 2:43 AM and finished at 3:03 AM*

Here you are on the
stage of your life.
How will your
performance go?
Will there be a
standing ovation because
of your passion,
or does stage fright
keep you captive
in the wings,
wanting to go out there,
but your knees are weak,
and your Spirit is unwilling?

Nerves freeze you in your tracks.
You don't have to perform alone.
Angels can whisper
lines in your ear and
thaw out those icy nerves.
Help surrounds you,
but no one comes
if you don't cooperate.

Ask for assistance.
Natural law and
free will mean we
show up on life's stage
the way we choose.

Did you study your part
and memorize your lines?
Did you pay attention
when the director explained
the scene and blocking?

Do you know how to interact
with your fellow actors?
On the stage of your life,
there are no dark times
at the theatre.
All performances take place,
and the theatre
opens every night.

The actors show up ready
for the opening curtain.
This is your moment.
You aren't in rehearsals anymore.
You apply the makeup and
put on your costume.
Artists paint the scenery,
and the staff sells tickets.

The audience awaits
your performance.
They have heard the reviews
and enthusiasm builds.
Will you show up on time
and deliver your lines
with conviction?

Will you cover for fellow actors
if they get confused and
lost in the script?

You are all in this show
of life together,
so if you support one another,
it will benefit all.

We look forward to
your performance.
If you have fun, embody
your character, and deliver
your lines with conviction,
we'll join in, and your
fantasy and drama
will become our story, too.

When you reach out and
include us in your performance
by inviting us in, you give us
courage to show up when it
becomes our turn to
be on the stage.

# RAW

Has this world left you
feeling raw, unprotected,
and way too emotional?
Do news events, feelings
of strife, unrest, protest,
fear, and anger stir up
jangled emotions, exposed nerves,
and unresolved feelings
about many things?

Do you feel raw, sad,
confused, and fearful about
the political climate,
global warming, and
changing weather patterns?
Are you raw with
emotion and fear about
new viruses and illnesses,
which seem so out of control?

Are you raw from
your own personal tragedy,
like the unexpected passing of
a loved one, a sick child,
extra financial pressures,
bad news, failure to
fill-in-the-blank?

Are you raw because
you feel unprotected
and ill-equipped to deal
with changes in our world?

When you feel raw, you
access feelings and
experience your humanity.
You may need to feel raw
to stir up emotions
and jolt you out
of your complacent life.

Rawness propels you
forward and helps you
experience oneness.
Mistreatment or unfairness
of one group of people
means inequality for all.

Privilege and tradition
must be dismantled for you
to see the connection underneath.
Rawness itself is unsustainable
and must yield to unity,
relief, softness, and peace.

Pure raw nerves and minds
cannot tolerate a frightened state
for too long, so you must
feel those feelings,
experience those emotions,
and accept that they are
simply feelings in motion.

As they pass through,
they don't have to
overwhelm you.
You must pray, meditate,
get quiet, go within,
seek beauty in nature,
and peace for your soul.

Connect to God
and the angels, which
is balm on a wound.
While you're in the rawness,
God comforts and
sustains you.
He covers you with love,
as you are
blanketed in peace.

You sink into reverie
with Him in the stillness
of your meditation,
in the warmth of
a friend's embrace,
in the laugh and
unexpected humor of
your funny friend,
in the giggle of a
young child who experiences joy
in the wonders of life,
the constant connection
with your sibling,
or the ever-faithful love and
support from your spouse.

Rawness may come, and
you will experience it.
Don't drown yourself
in the rawness, but
let it inform, mold, and
move you to healing,
health, compassion,
and connection with
the Prince of Peace,
the Source of all,
the Creator who connects all,
and creates Oneness.

# CELEBRATION

# TRIUMPH

*Started at 3:36 AM and finished at 3:53 AM*

Will you triumph over yourself?
Can you set aside petty worries
and dive into life's flow?
Jump into the juice, and
let it stream all over you.
Let it wake, shake, and
rattle you out
of your doldrums.

Will you join in the parade?
Can you lead it like
a high-strutting drum major
marching down the field?
Be loud, proud, and
celebrate your life.
Make noise, create mistakes,
be a loud spectator,
and cheer others on.
Celebrate life instead of
sulking on the sidelines,
sad that you dropped
your popcorn and worried
that you missed something.

The only thing you
missed is yourself.
This is your time, moment,
and chance to enjoy

the thrills and spills.
Throw the confetti,
sound the trumpet,
beat the cadence
on the snare drum.
Join the twirlers
as they throw their
batons in the air and turn
cartwheels with the gymnasts.

This is your glorious life,
time, and moment
to sparkle, shine,
and twinkle like the light
that's deep inside you.
When you let yours out,
you encourage others
to stop hiding theirs.

Have fun, play music,
and do the dance steps
as you strut down Main Street.
Celebrate your glory.
Share your radiance.
We need you.
We want you.
We're counting on you.
All parade people matter.

We're in this together.
The quiet ones and

boisterous ones,
jugglers and children,
party-throwers and face painters,
animal lovers and scaredy cats.

We need every single one
because some fantastic color
will be missing,
if you don't show up.
Don't wait for an invitation.
Jump right out into
the sea of humanity
as the parade passes you.
Don't wait too long
to join the celebration.
Your purpose is joy, pleasure,
and the whole messy middle.

You don't have to
know the steps or
plan the choreography.
Blend with the band or
create your own tune.
All expressions are welcome.
Don't wait on the sidelines.
We need you now.
We want you, too.

# LAUGHING

*Started at 6:54 AM and finished at 7:01 AM*

Laughing is a
passport to paradise.
Hear the tinkling bells.
Taste the elixir that
fills you with joy.
Transport yourself
into others and give
yourself new possibilities.

Laughter ripples
through the crowd,
lightening the spirit
of the room.
Laughter is the
magician who shifts us,
shapes us, and moves us
to higher planes.

Laughing is the language
of children who discover
joy and silliness
in simple things.
A child's laugh captivates
and weaves the stuff of angels
into everyday activities.

Laughing shakes us
out of our seriousness
and delivers a gift.
When was the last time
you let yourself laugh out loud?

# WHAT ARE YOU WAITING FOR?

*Started at 4:07 AM and finished at 4:17 AM*

What are you waiting for?
Are you waiting for
the stars to set,
the planets to align,
the clarion call, or
the delivery at your door?

Come now and join in the fun.
Play in the puddles and
splash through the rain.
Let your glasses get
splattered and foggy,
so you can't see,
but you laugh anyway.

What are you waiting for?
Are you looking for
the right time
or certain people?
Do you need
permission from yourself
or an omniscient judge?
Are you waiting
for someone to lead you
by the hand like some
frightened schoolgirl
on her first day in class?

Let yourself go.
The time is right, or
you will make it right.
Dance, draw, paint,
write, figure, or design
your devotion and your prayers,
your triumphs, failures,
losses, and leaps of faith.
Tumble into the mess and
jump into the middle.

If you wait for
the perfect moment,
the prize, the applause,
or the grandeur,
you'll never go.
Just throw yourself in there,
out there, and fully there.

We need you, so join us.
When we're chattering like
kids on a new adventure,
we make a joyful crowd.
Don't wait.
Come now.
We're here.
We're ready.
Will you join?

# STAINED-GLASS WINDOWS

*Started at 4:24 AM and finished at 4:33 AM*

What makes color in
stained-glass windows vibrant,
bright, and breathtaking?
Is it the combination
of blues and reds,
greens and golds,
ochres and orange,
indigo and marbled white?
Is it figures, geometry, saints,
animals, the Holy Family, or angels?

What makes stained-glass windows
so captivating?
Is it the way the artist
laid the pieces side-by-side
or found the right hue
to convey a tone or shade?
Stained-glass windows
offer riotous color,
thrill our senses, and
delight our spirits.

What makes stained-glass windows
burst with beauty?
It's the light.
Transformation occurs
when sunlight pours through.
Colors blaze out,

rainbows adorn the floor,
and a kaleidoscope
of designs appears.
The light is the magic
in stained-glass windows,
and it's the magic in you, too.

# THE GLASS CONTAINER

*Started at 4:59 AM and finished at 5:15 AM*

What is displayed in the
glass container in your room?
Are there colorful M&M's
like your granny
used to keep as a treat?
As hard as she was
on herself and others,
what a delight to see those
little gems beckon the
one who needed a little
sweetness in her life.

Is your glass container
chock full of seashells
and beach glass you collected
on a special trip to the shore?
Does it evoke happiness and
nostalgia for you to
see those magical little
treasures from the sea?

Is that glass container filled
with your grandfather's
collection of marbles,
the kind they don't
make anymore?
The cat's eyes and
colorful spheres that

almost seem like their own
little planets trapped in
a moment in time.

Does that glass container
warehouse buttons,
antique ones,
new shiny ones, and
little delicate ones, so
colorful and abundant
that they appear to be exotic
ancient coins used
for barter and trade?

Does that glass container
store little white butter mints
or unusual white ones
with green soft centers
that your piano teacher
keeps on her coffee table?
If you can carefully
slip off the lid,
she won't know you
took a piece as you
wait for the student
before you to finish.

Is the glass container full of
those little Matchbox cars
that you used to race around
the kitchen floor for hours?
Is it full of beautiful dried flowers
or fragrant potpourri?

Is it spilling over with
beads and baubles for
an art project you create?
Is the glass container full of
paint brushes of different sizes?
Or is it stocked with markers,
so you can draw a treasure map,
a mind map, or a vision board
that sparks your imagination as
you transport yourself out of a
mediocre automatic-pilot life into
a fantasy land of your own making?

A glass container may hold simple,
ordinary items, but it is
the memories and creativity
it evokes in you that
make all the difference.

# HARVEST

*Started at 5:16 AM and finished at 5:38 AM*

Are you in the
harvest time now?
How have you been
spending your time?
You will reap what you sow.
Are you reaping kindness
because you spread it to others?

Are you reaping patience
because you demonstrate it?
Are you harvesting joy
because you uplift others
with your bright spirit?

Are you reaping new growth
in your intuition because
you tune in, ask for help, and
respond to inner urges?

Are you reaping love
because you embody it?
Are you reaping freedom
because you pay attention
to what's a *yes* for you,
and you're bold to say *no*?

Are you harvesting peace of mind
because you stopped obsessing

about the news and things
out of your control?
Do you harvest friendship
because you click with
someone new and
support each other?

Do you harvest health
because you listen to your body,
and pay attention to what
you're eating and drinking?
Do you exercise your body
because it needs to move?

Are you harvesting the
results of your creativity?
New recipes, fancy table decorations,
clothes you sewed, or
the art project you created?
Does your creativity include:
a painting, a children's book you wrote,
or adorable animals you sketched
to illustrate a story?

What about the dance
you choreographed,
the song you wrote,
the poem you scratched
on a scrap of paper,
or the journal entries
you turned into a blog?

All these things are the gift of you.
When you invest in your passion,
you harvest something beautiful.
Where do you invest yourself?
Do you get pulled into
people or projects, which
hold no value for you?
This is your life, so don't
squander your precious time.

Consider the harvest.
Imagine what you
want to celebrate.
Where do you give
your heart, soul, and effort?
Every minute counts.
What do you want to harvest?
Are you committed to doing
what needs to be done?

# REDISCOVER

*Started at 2:45 AM and finished at 3:21 AM*

Rediscover the gift
of life when you have
fresh eyes with which to see.
Rediscover the joy of
learning as you allow yourself
to have a beginner's mind.

Rediscover the thrill
of a new day
as you cultivate
the practice of gratitude.
Rediscover the newness
of a relationship
as you continue to
be curious about each other.

Rediscover the pleasure
of being in someone's company
when you ask for
what you want
without demanding it
or without assuming the
other person should
already know what
you need or want.

Rediscover yourself by
getting out of the bad

neighborhood of gossip
and rumor mongering.

Rediscover the sweetness
of creating a day that
lifts your spirits and
allows you to feel nurtured,
loved, and attended to because
you check-in with your spirit
on what it wants to do today
instead of forcing yourself to
stay in a rut of repetitive living.

Rediscover your little child within
when you examine what you
loved to do as a young person.

Did you organize the
other kids in games?
Did you write clues
for a treasure hunt?
Did you play dress up, or
put on plays and shows
for anyone who would watch?

Were you the doctor
who cured your stuffed animals
or the artist who drew
to occupy her time?
Did you voraciously
consume books?
Did you sit on the back steps
singing songs about
everything in your life?

Did you explore your
neighborhood and collect
rocks, leaves, twigs, bugs,
and organize them into collections?
Did you run non-stop
night and day?
Did you sit on the sidelines,
observing and figuring things out
while others were running
around being busy?

Did you play in the garden
with the flower fairies making
little homes and play spaces
out of your imagination?

Were you the kid who
took everything apart because
you needed to see how it worked?
Did you feel everything
going on around you,
so you withdrew
to get quiet and
come back to yourself?

Did you like to entertain
your friends and family
with magic tricks or
surprise your mom and dad
with pancakes and coffee
for a special occasion breakfast?

Were you the girl whose mom
let her play in the kitchen,

mixing all the spices so you
could become your own chef?
As a child, you knew what
lit you up and
what gave you joy.

If you spent hours
dancing in your room,
or created fashion for paper dolls,
and colored clothes from stencil sets,
then you can rediscover
that spark again.

Revisit that childhood
part of you.

If you've lost yourself
in adult responsibilities
of family, work, home,
and all those grown-up things
we think are so important,
do yourself a favor and
remember what thrilled you
as a young person.

If you were the guy
who loved Halloween,
and couldn't wait to
plan next year's costume
while your stash
of Halloween candy
was untouched this year,
maybe you want to join
friends at Comic Con
or visit sick kids

in the hospital
as a superhero.

If you're the child who
organized toys and clothes
and wanted to do the
same for others,
maybe you will become
a professional organizer.

Whatever it is that
grounded you,
sparked your creativity,
and swept you away
for hours in flow,
rediscover that lost part
of yourself and you win
the biggest prize.

Nothing can hold you back now.

# RESOURCES

Also by Betsy Brown Bass and Susan Beris, M.D. – *Beyond the Visit*

Sonia Choquette (www.soniachoquette.net) – Spiritual teacher, Intuitive Mentor, Best-selling author of books, oracle cards and courses. Podcast: "It's All Related" with her daughters, Sonia and Sabrina.

Vishen Lakhiani – Founder and CEO of www.mindvalley.com. *The Code of the Extraordinary Mind* (2016) and *The Buddha and the Badass* (2020)

Brené Brown (www.brenebrown.com) – author, speaker, teacher. *The Gifts of Imperfection* (2010), *Daring Greatly* (2012), *Rising Strong* (2015), *Braving the Wilderness* (2017), *Dare to Lead* (2018), *Atlas of the Heart* (2021) Podcast: "Unlocking Us"

SARK (Susan Ariel Rainbow Kennedy) – artist, author, speaker, teacher. www.planetsark.com

Samantha Bennett (www.TheRealSamBennett.com) *Get it Done* (2014), *Start Right Where You Are* (2016).

Rebecca Campbell (www.rebeccacampbell.me), author, artist, teacher, creator of oracle cards.
"Rise Sister Rise" membership site. *Light is the New Black* (2015), *Rise Sister Rise* (2016), *Letters to a Starseed* (2021)

Rebecca Rosen (www.rebeccarosen.com) – medium, author, teacher. "Spirited" written with Samantha Rose. Podcast: "Small Medium at Large"

Lee Harris (www.leeharrisenergy.com) – Energy Intuitive and Transformation Guide, Musician. Online courses, downloads and membership site.

Julia Cameron (www.juliacameronlive.com) – Teacher, author, artist, composer. *The Artist's Way* (1992)

Flora Bowley (www.florabowley.com) – Artist, author, creative pioneer. *Brave Intuitive Painting* (2012), *Creative Revolution* (2016), *The Art of Aliveness* (2021)

Lynzee Lynx (www.yourstrangefriend.com) – Artist, jewelry maker, teacher. *Fresh Paint* written with Flora Bowley (2021)

Leslie Helpert (www.dynamicvoicetraining.com) – Vocal coach, musician, composer, artist, author.

Robert Holden (www.robertholden.com) – author, teacher, psychologist.

Hollie Holden (www.hollieholden.me) – artist, teacher, group leader. Robert and Hollie Holden host an annual study of "A Course in Miracles" (www.2022. everydaymiracles.love)

Jennifer Currie (www.jennifercurrie.com) – Artist, intuitive coach.

# ACKNOWLEDGMENTS

I have been inspired by many people over the years, and I first want to acknowledge all of my teachers, especially Sonia Choquette, with whom I have studied since 2010. She is an incredible teacher, mentor, and role model. Sonia challenges her students to grow and is generous as she shares her knowledge while being completely authentic in her own evolution. In the early 1980s, I discovered SARK, (Susan Ariel Rainbow Kennedy) and was completely enthralled with her bold use of color and deep dive into creativity. In several poems, I refer to the "messy middle" of our lives, and I wanted to make sure that I credit SARK for the use of the term, which I find to be very descriptive. I received training from Andrrea Hess in reading the Akashic Records, and for that I am grateful. In 2021, I started a year-long journey into *A Course in Miracles* led by Robert and Hollie Holden, and their love, warmth, and sense of community encourages my connection to God.

I also want to thank my editor and designer, Heather Dakota, for her help in getting this book from rough form out into the world. Her experience and direction have been invaluable. Thanks to my coach, Jennifer Currie, artist and creative, whose compassion and skill have helped me evolve. Leslie Helpert, friend, voice coach, writer, deep-thinker, and wildly creative person continues to inspire me in ways I probably do not even realize. Thanks also to my voice teacher, Alexa Vogelzang Brown, who helps me express joy in singing. Thanks to all my friends and fellow performers at Moonlight Musicals in Lubbock for giving me an opportunity to share the stage. I want to thank Flora Bowley for teaching me to paint boldly on large canvases, and to her fellow artist, Lynzee Lynx, who was so loving and encouraging during our workshop in Portland, Oregon.

I also want to thank friends from a year-long support group I led connected with Sonia Choquette's course, "Your Glorious Life." Thanks to Shannon, Judy, Paz, Kathleen, and especially Kimberly, who eagerly awaited my new poems almost as much as I did. Kimberly was enthusiastic and supportive throughout the entire month I was writing. Thanks to Jordana Borensztajn from Australia who was in a small Mentoring Group led by Sonia Choquette. Her great sense of humor and light-hearted joy remind me not to take myself too seriously. I also want to acknowledge Rebecca Campbell, Hay House author and good friend, along with other students of Sonia Choquette, Monika Laschkolnig, Susanne Snellman, Fiona Radman, and Sanja Plavljanic-Sirola who shared their dreams with me in an international Mastermind group. Thanks to Leland Arnsdorff who attended Sonia's training with me and has always championed my creative endeavors.

A huge thanks to Bonnie Hill, coaching colleague and fantastically nurturing friend, who always "gets" me.

Everyone needs a friend like Bonnie Hill. Thanks also to Anne Durand, MCC, who was my coach and teacher at MentorCoach and gave me an opportunity to be a trainer. Anne encouraged me to get in touch with my intuition before it became a popular topic. Thanks to Carol Solomon, Ph.D and Jeff Kaplan, Ph.D, psychologists and fellow coaches, who helped me develop my skills. Thanks to an amazing group of friends, The Morningstars, who attended a year-long leadership training course through CTI in Santa Rosa, California with me in 2003. I felt especially supported by my roommate and travel companion, Madelyn Roche, and by Robert Giambrone, Jim Bower, Phil Hoch, and Anese Cavanaugh. I also wish to thank my friend, Susan Ross, who has shared life's journey, especially related to parenting and personal development. Her wisdom and insights have been a gift to me. I want to acknowledge my good friend, colleague, and child psychiatrist in Connecticut, John Gelinas, M.D., who is a force for good and who trusted me with the families he was helping. I am grateful to all the clients and people who have allowed me into their lives and to the clients I have yet to meet. I also want to give a big thanks to Terri Blassingame, Lubbock friend and Reiki Master, whose intuition and playfulness bless me.

Thanks to my friend Dr. Callie Kostelich, Assistant Professor and Acting Writing Program Administrator at Texas Tech University, who enthusiastically edited my introduction. I am indebted to friends Serafina, Theresa, Luisa, Caden, Isabella, Belinda, and Samuel for their guidance in bringing this poetry to the world. Thanks to my twin sister, Bonnie Jump, for helping me first organize the poems and also to my sister, Gretchen Walker, and brother, Richard Brown, for their support.

I am grateful to my son, Chris, daughter, Camille, and granddaughter, Liesl, for their interest in hearing what I had to say. Their opinions matter to me. I am especially thankful for my husband, Mark, who is my greatest gift and who loves and encourages me to be myself in all endeavors, large and small. Thanks also to God, my guides, angels, unseen helpers, ancestors, and beings of light who help us everyday in many ways. In advance, I want to express my gratitude to all the people who read this poetry, and I pray that it will encourage and inspire you to create the joyous lives you want to live.

# ABOUT THE AUTHOR

Betsy Bass is a Life Coach, Intuitive Healer, and Creative Spirit. She has more than 40 years combined experience as a Marriage, Family, and Child Therapist and coach. Betsy's love of beauty and dedication to living a vibrant life inspires everything she does. She's multilingual, has lived on both coasts and in the middle of the country, enjoys travel, and constantly explores new ways to express her creativity from singing and dancing to painting, drawing, and writing. Since 2014, she has become passionate about performing in musicals. She combines her grounded expertise as a coach with Reiki and Akashic Record wisdom to guide those seeking a deeper connection to their intuition, creative expression, and abundant living. Betsy is very happily married to her husband, Mark, and they live in Lubbock, Texas.

Learn more at www.betsybass.com